# DIGITAL MARKETING

# For Beginners 2022

A Comprehensive Guide to Online marketing, Locating Your Customers, and expanding your Business Profitably

## Todd A. Holmes

# CONTENTS

# INTRODUCTION

Online marketing and digital marketing are sometimes conflated. The process of promoting a brand, service, or product via the internet is known as digital marketing. Simply said, digital marketing varies from traditional marketing in that it employs internet channels and methods to allow businesses and organizations to track the effectiveness of their marketing campaigns, frequently in real time, in order to better understand what works and what doesn't. Most businesses have developed a web presence in the twenty-first century. E-mail was widely used, and technology enabled users to manage it relatively effortlessly.

For a long time, databases were managed using customer relationship management (CRM) systems. Some corporations used a similar strategy to press advertising by displaying banners on websites. Forward-thinking businesses were developing their search engine strategies and even collaborating with affiliates. This was all internet marketing, and online marketing teams and professionals would emerge over time. 2016 (Kingsnorth). The most popular type of digital marketing is the organization's website, which serves as the hub for all of the organization's online activity. Email marketing, search engine optimization (SEO), pay-per-click (PPC) advertising, and social media are all used by sophisticated marketers to attract quality traffic to a website or encourage repeat visitors and transactions.

# CHAPTER ONE

# WHAT IS DIGITAL MARKETING?

Digital marketing was first characterized as a projection of traditional marketing, including its tools and techniques, onto the Internet (Otero and Rolan, 2016). It is known as 'online marketing,' 'web marketing,' or 'internet marketing,' according to Satya (2015). Digital marketing grew in popularity over time, particularly in certain countries. Online marketing is still popular in the United States, and web marketing is used in Italy, but digital marketing has become the most used phrase in the United Kingdom and around the world, especially since 2013. Digital marketing refers to the promotion of products or services through the use of digital technology, such as the Internet, but also mobile phones, display advertising, and other digital words.

## Definition of marketing strategy

Different organizations utilize marketing strategies to collaborate with their customers. It's also used to inform customers about the company's products' characteristics, specifications, and benefits. Its main goal is to persuade the target audience to purchase certain items and services. The marketing methods may be completely new or may have been tried and proven previously.

## Effective marketing techniques

The marketing methods may be completely new or may have been tried and proven previously.

## Consider these marketing considerations

There are numerous marketing tactics to choose from. You must choose one based on your company's needs. Consider the following factors before deciding on the best marketing approach for your company.

### 1. Determine the target demographic.

The first and most important step in deciding on a marketing plan is to define your target audience. It provides accurate demographics that aid in the selection of the best marketing strategy for your company.

## 2. Perform audience research

To test your audience, create a fictional buying process. You can choose a more appropriate marketing plan after you understand your target audience's buying habits.

## 3. Think about marketing techniques.

Once you have a good understanding of the demographics, including their knowledge, attitudes, and behaviors. You can choose a more effective marketing plan.

## 4. Assess the strategies.

After you've considered marketing tactics and determined which ones are appropriate, Assess, implement, and evaluate them. This procedure must be used for testing, and the most appropriate and productive method must be used.

## Types of Marketing strategies

There are numerous marketing tactics to choose from. Choosing a marketing plan entails assessing your company's needs, your target audience, and product specs.

*There are two sorts of marketing strategies:*

1. B2B (business-to-business) marketing
2. B2C (business-to-consumer) marketing

Business to consumer (B2C) marketing is the most popular type of marketing. Let's dig a little deeper.

## What are various sorts of marketing tactics

### 1. Paid promotion

This involves a variety of marketing strategies. Traditional methods such as television commercials and print media advertising are included. In addition, internet marketing is a well-known marketing strategy. It includes techniques such as pay-per-click (PPC) and paid advertising.

## 2. Social marketing

Cause marketing connects a company's services and goods to a social cause or issue. Cause-related marketing is another term for it.

## 3. Marketing through relationships

Customer acquisition is the primary goal of this sort of marketing. Increasing consumer loyalty and enhancing existing customer connections.

## 4. Marketing undercover

Customers are uninformed of the marketing strategy; hence this type of marketing strategy concentrates on marketing the product. Stealth marketing is another term for it.

## 5. Personal recommendation

It is entirely dependent on the impression you make on others. It is the most essential form of marketing strategy in the past. In the commercial world, it is critical to be heard. Customers are more inclined to promote you if you provide them with high-quality services.

## 6. Internet promotion

Cloud marketing is another name for it. It mainly occurs through the internet. All marketing materials are shared on the internet and pushed across many platforms using various methods.

## 7. **Transactional marketing Sales**

is one of the most difficult jobs to perform. Even for the largest stores, selling is difficult, especially when volume targets are high. Selling is no longer as difficult as it once was thanks to modern marketing methods. Customers are encouraged to buy using shopping coupons, discounts, and large events in transactional marketing. It increases the likelihood of sales and encourages the target audience to purchase the advertised products.

### 8. Market diversity

It serves to a wide range of customers by developing and merging various marketing methods. It covers several characteristics such as cultural, beliefs, attitudes, and viewpoints, as well as other special requirements.

## How Is Marketing Strategy Different from Marketing Tactics or Campaigns?

Marketing tactics differ from marketing strategy in that they indicate the exact activities or actions required to attain those aims. It is vital to develop tactics as part of the marketing strategy development process in order to define the plan and timescales. Otherwise, successfully executing a marketing plan and achieving marketing goals may be challenging, if not impossible.

In this topic, digital marketing campaigns are also important to assess. These digital campaigns entail putting marketing tactics into action across all of a company's digital channels. The marketing methods utilized to carry out these campaigns are frequently different depending on the channel, audience, and other considerations. However, a successful digital marketing campaign will have a consistent message across all mediums.

## Some Examples of Digital Marketing Techniques

There are numerous digital marketing approaches available, which are frequently adjusted to match the needs of different organizations and marketing plans. However, there are a few typical digital marketing strategies that many businesses use successfully, including:

- Search Engine Optimization (SEO) – SEO is the process of improving material in order to increase search engine rankings. Organizations can better reach prospective customers through major search engines by following standard SEO strategies with all digital material.

- **Social Media Marketing (SMM)** – SMM is the process of reaching out to customers and communicating corporate messaging through social media networks. Customers can be reached directly through their preferred social channel by businesses who effectively use SMM methods.

- **Digital Advertising** — Digital advertising is the practice of placing firm advertisements in numerous internet areas, such as search engines and social media networks. Digital advertising includes paid placement in search results and pop-up ads.

- **Pay-Per-Click (PPC) Advertising** – PPC advertising is a type of digital advertising in which businesses publish ads on a third-party website in order to drive visitors to their site. Companies only pay for PPC advertising when a user clicks on the link, unlike other forms of advertising.

- **Content Marketing —** Content marketing is the process of targeting prospective customers through a company's own media platforms. Companies that regularly generate and publish high-quality content can enhance their rankings and increase traffic to their website.

- **Website Promotion —** A company's website is an immensely strong weapon in the realm of content marketing. An organization can become a thought leader in their sector and attract potential customers with strong call-to-action messages by establishing geo-targeted and optimized landing pages.

- **Email Marketing** – Used to increase customer relationships or drive engagement with a current or future audience. Email marketing services are a powerful instrument that has a track record of success.
- **Downloadable Content** – Downloadable content is a subset of website strategy that is an effective technique to generate leads. Companies may provide high-quality content that prospects can download for free, while also collecting valuable contact information.

Organizations use a variety of marketing tactics on a daily basis, when taken as a whole. Successful marketers can clearly identify goals and then select appropriate tactics to achieve those goals while staying focused on the overall strategy, business needs, and budget constraints.

# How Do I Create a Successful Digital Marketing Strategy?

Following this five-step method can help you establish an efficient digital marketing plan, as explained further below:

1. Conduct a SWOT analysis;
2. Establish SMART company goals;
3. Engage in market segmentation;
4. Develop buyer personas; and
5. Determine financial restrictions.

1. **SWOT analysis** is an abbreviation for Strengths, Weaknesses, Opportunities, and Threats, and it is a cornerstone of marketing strategy. SWOT encompasses both internal (strengths/weaknesses) and external (opportunities/threats) components from this perspective:

- **Strengths —** Strengths are internal factors that enable businesses to meet and maybe exceed their objectives. High sales and profits, customer loyalty, long-term staff, and an appealing brand/culture are all examples of strengths.

- **Weaknesses** – Weaknesses are internal obstacles that impede companies from achieving their objectives. Improperly advertised products or services, frequent consumer complaints, high levels of personnel turnover, insufficient funding, or supply chain concerns are all examples of shortcomings.

- **Opportunities** – Opportunities are external conditions that have the potential to help an organization prosper in the future. Changing attitudes or aspirations, new laws or regulations, trade agreements, or tariffs/sanctions removal are all examples of opportunity.

- **Threats** – Threats are external conditions that have the potential to harm an organization in the future. Shifts in the labor market, rising supply costs, and new competition/technology are all examples of threats.

## 2. Set SMART Business Objectives

SMART refers to corporate goals that are Specific, Measurable, Attainable, Relevant, and Timely, and is another prominent acronym in the marketing strategy arena. Organizations may guarantee that their marketing strategy is moving in the right way by setting SMART business goals.

### What to consider as a Marketers and leaders when setting SMART business goals

- **Specific —** What am I aiming to achieve, why is it important, and what will be required?
- **Measurable –** How will I be able to track and assess my progress in order to fulfill deadlines and achieve my ultimate goal?
- **Achievable –** Is the end aim genuinely attainable given the available resources and constraints?

- Is the final aim valuable at this time, given current business needs/reality and the general environment?
- **On time** – When can I expect to see results? What advantages can be expected right now versus in the short, medium, or long term?

### 3. Use market segmentation techniques.

A successful digital marketing plan frequently includes market segmentation. This method entails segmenting a company's target market or audience into smaller groups. It becomes easier to design distinct marketing techniques to each market segment by segmenting an entire client base into manageable chunks.

**Four Categories of Organizations when it comes to market segmentation**:

- **Demographic** — In the business-to-consumer (B2C) setting, demographic segmentation focuses on personal traits. Demographic segmentation divides clients into groups based on criteria such as age, education, gender, and location.

- **Firmographic segmentation** focuses on organizational features and is used in the business-to-business (B2B) environment. Firmographic segmentation divides firms into categories based on variables such as revenue, industry, location, and employee count.

- **Psychographic segmentation** – Psychographic segmentation can happen in both B2C and B2B situations. Psychographic egmentation looks at things like personality, opinions, ambitions, and lifestyle to categorize prospects.

- **Behavioral** — Behavioral segmentation can happen in both B2C and B2B scenarios. To categorize prospects, behavioral segmentation looks at things like purchasing history, brand loyalty, and usage trends.

## 4. Develop buyer personas.

Buyer personas are fictional profiles that reflect the client and are frequently used in conjunction with market segmentation. Buyer personas are very useful for understanding a company's customers, whether they are current, prospective, or desired. Buyer personas, on the other hand, differ significantly from sector to industry and organization to organization. As previously stated, marketers frequently combine buyer personas with market segmentation efforts. Marketers aim to develop ideal consumer profiles based on demographic, firmographic, psychographic, and behavioral data in this way. As a result, businesses may tailor their messaging, products, and services to each consumer persona and market group separately.

## 5. Determine your financial constraints

Fundamentally, all commercial and charitable organizations must spend appropriately in order to implement an efficient digital marketing plan.

Even the most effective marketing strategy and approaches are contingent on sufficient financial flow. As a result, it is critical for businesses to consider their budget in order to identify which marketing methods are feasible and cheap.

## Digital Marketing Strategy that is Right for your Business?

The components of an excellent digital marketing plan can differ significantly from one company to the next. After all, variances in culture, product offers, revenue ambitions, and other factors will influence general business directives and specific marketing goals. Businesses of all shapes and sizes may profit from digital marketing by aligning diverse strategies and approaches with SMART business goals and segmented buyer personas. The exact rewards vary depending on how much time and money is spent on digital marketing techniques and tactics.

Digital marketing strategy for startups and small organizations would most likely rely on cost-effective techniques to accomplish organizational goals. These businesses may achieve their digital marketing objectives at a reasonable cost by utilizing SEO, social media marketing, and content marketing. Because of the low entrance barrier and low expense of these methods, businesses of all shapes and sizes can benefit. Organizations' marketing and advertising costs often grow in lockstep with their growth. As a result, by combining marketing, advertising, and public/investor relations initiatives, the potential benefits from effective marketing approaches can grow enormously. When all of this is considered, firms who devote substantial budget and resources to digital marketing can reap significant benefits.

## HOW HAS DIGITAL MARKETING EVOLVED?

The internet and consumer behavior have been fundamentally transformed by the social media revolution. With over 40% of the world being online and over 90% in several places, board-band penetration has increased speed, internet consumption, and consumer expectations (Internet World Stats, 2015). We can now understand our customers' activity in real time, including not just their usage statistics but also their demographics and even their interests, thanks to advances in analytics. Mobile phones have become smarter, and tablets have exploded onto the scene, bringing with them apps. Touchscreens are becoming more common on all types of gadgets. Google has grown into a massive corporation that controls the global search market. Smart TVs have here, and Bluetooth adds another layer of functionality. With a naturally aging population, only a small fraction of people are technophobic due to their age. The use of digital media to reach consumers in order to promote items or services. The main goal is to promote brands using different types of digital media. Digital marketing includes outlets that do not require the use of the internet in addition to internet marketing.

Mobile phones (SMS and MMS), social media marketing, display advertising, search engine marketing, and any other kind of digital media are all included. Most experts believe that "digital" is more than just another marketing channel. It necessitates a new marketing strategy as well as a new understanding of customer behavior. Companies must, for example, analyze and quantify the value of app downloads on mobile devices, tweets on Twitter, Facebook likes, and so on. An effective digital marketing campaign example Pizza Hut ran a successful digital media campaign in which customers could construct their own pizza by dragging their preferred toppings onto a graphical pizza foundation. The iPhone would then figure out which of the chain's thousands of stores was closest to the customer. The company promoted the new software on the web, in print, and on television, even landing a spot in an Apple advertisement.

 The Pizza Hut app was downloaded 100,000 times in two weeks, and iPhone users ordered $1 million worth of pizza in three months. On the iPhone, iPad, and Android platforms, the app now has millions of users. All marketing approaches are used to digital channels in digital marketing. SMS, search engines, email, websites, social media, and mobile devices can all be used to promote services and products. Because of the digital nature of this marketing approach, it is a cost-effective way to promote a firm. 2016 (Kingsnorth) The utilization of digital marketing is determined by the marketing goals of the company. It's possible that the company aims to increase lead generation, brand awareness, revenue, or brand engagement.

Having a website isn't enough for digital marketing.

The website must be visually appealing and simple to access, as well as contain high-quality information that reflects the nature of the business. Another crucial issue is search engine optimization (SEO). The webpage must be correctly read and indexed by search engines. There are content and SEO experts who can assist businesses in creating responsive websites that can be visited on any device. In addition to managing the company's social media presence and communicating with fans, digital marketing include marketing the company via key social media networks.

# CHAPTER 2

# DIGITAL MARKETING'S HISTORY AND EVOLUTION

Every working professional should be familiar with at least the key ideas of Digital Marketing in a world where over 170 million individuals use social media on a regular basis. Digital marketing, to put it simply, is the advertising of items using the internet or other forms of electronic media. "Digital marketing is the use of digital platforms to promote or advertise products and services to targeted consumers and businesses," according to the Digital Marketing Institute. On a daily basis, people consume digital content. Traditional marketing platforms will soon be obsolete, and the internet market will entirely dominate. Digital marketing has a variety of benefits. Digital marketing is less expensive than traditional marketing. In a shorter amount of time, you may reach a wider audience. Traditional marketing organizations and departments have seen significant customer churn as a result of technological advancements. People have shifted to tablets, phones, and laptops, which are where digital marketers have made the most progress. In the 1990s, the phrase "digital marketing" was coined. With the introduction of the internet and the creation of the Web 1.0 platform, the digital age began. Users could find the information they needed on the Web 1.0 platform, but they couldn't share it. Marketers all around the world were still apprehensive about the digital platform at the time.

They weren't sure if their plans would work because the internet hadn't been widely adopted yet. The first clickable banner was launched in 1993, and Hotwired bought a few banner ads for their advertising. This was the start of the transition to the digital marketing era. As a result of this gradual transformation, new technologies entered the digital marketplace in 1994. Yahoo was founded in the same year. After its founder Jerry Yang, Yahoo was dubbed "Jerry's Guide to the World Wide Web" and received about 1 million hits in its first year. As a result, the digital marketing landscape has changed dramatically, with businesses improving their websites to achieve higher search engine ranks. HotBot, LookSmart, and Alexa were among the search engines and tools that debuted in 1996.

Google was founded in 1998. Microsoft released the MSN search engine, while Yahoo released Yahoo web search. The internet bubble burst two years later, and all of the smaller search engines were either left behind or wiped out, leaving more room for the industry's behemoths. In 2006, search engine traffic was claimed to have increased by 6.4 billion in a single month, marking the beginning of the digital marketing boom. Microsoft, not wanting to be left behind, placed MSN on hold and built Live Search to compete with Google and Yahoo. Then came Web 2.0, which encouraged individuals to become more active participants rather than passive consumers. Web 2.0 enabled people to communicate with one another and with businesses. The internet came to be labeled as a "super information highway." As a result, information flow volumes – including channels used by digital marketers – rose dramatically, and internet advertising and marketing in the United States alone brought in $2.9 billion by 2004. Social networking sites appeared soon after. The first social networking site to appear was Myspace, which was quickly followed by Facebook. Many businesses understood that all of these new websites were beginning to open up new avenues for marketing their products and brands. It opened up new business opportunities and marked the start of a new chapter in the commercial world. They required fresh techniques to market their businesses and capitalize on the social networking platform now that they had more resources.

Another significant milestone in the digital marketing business was the cookie. Advertisers were looking for alternative ways to profit from the new technology. One such strategy was to track frequent internet users' surfing activities and usage patterns in order to personalize promotions and marketing collateral to their preferences. The first cookie was created to keep track of user habits. Cookies have evolved over time, and they are now coded to provide advertisers with a number of ways to capture literal user data.

Customers can now access digitally advertised products at any time. According to Marketingtech 2014 statistics, posting on social media is the most popular online activity in the United States. The average person in the United States spends 37 minutes each day on social media. Facebook is used by 99 percent of digital marketers, while Twitter is used by 97 percent, Pinterest by 69 percent, and Instagram by 59 percent. Customers were acquired by 70% of B2C marketers on Facebook. 67 percent of Twitter users are more likely to buy from firms they follow on the social media platform. Pinterest accounts for 83.8 percent of luxury businesses. LinkedIn, Twitter, and Facebook are the top three social networking sites utilized by marketers.

## Difference between Traditional Marketing and Digital Marketing

Because their budget only allows for one or the other, many small businesses struggle to decide which type of marketing to pursue. The judgments that must be taken are difficult: which marketing approach will generate the most sales and profits? How can I tell whether my marketing is effective? Who should I put my marketing in the hands of? Should I take care of it myself? To clarify the concepts, conventional marketing is defined as the use of print advertisements in newspapers and periodicals. Other examples include leaflets placed in mailboxes, television and radio ads, and billboards. Digital marketing, on the other hand, is when a company spends in creating a website and advertising the brand name through various social media platforms such as Facebook, Twitter, and YouTube. Traditional Marketing's Advantages You can effortlessly reach your local target market. A radio commercial, for example, might only play in one location: your city or region. Alternatively, residents in a restricted number of suburbs will receive mailbox flyers. 8 The materials are safe to keep. The audience can get a hard copy of the information to read or browse through at their leisure. It's simple to comprehend.

Most people can understand it because they are already familiar with this type of method. Traditional Marketing's Drawbacks The relationship between the medium and the clients is minimal. It's more about informing the audience that the brand exists in the hopes that they will patronize the brand. Advertisements in print or on the radio can be highly expensive. It can be costly to print materials, and you will need to hire personnel to deliver them. This marketing strategy's results are difficult to quantify. Was your campaign a success? Digital Marketing's Advantages You can target both a local and an international audience. You can also target a campaign to certain demographics like gender, geography, age, and hobbies. As a result, your campaign will be more successful. Your audience has the option of receiving your content in a variety of ways. While one person enjoys reading blog posts, another enjoys watching YouTube videos. The audience is not given a choice in traditional marketing. Most people despise getting sales brochures in the mail or phone calls at inconvenient times about products they don't want. People who use the internet have the option of opting in or out of communications, which is often relevant because they were looking for it in the first place.

The utilization of social media networks allows you to interact with your audience. Interaction is actually encouraged. Audience contact is not possible with traditional marketing approaches. You may encourage your prospects, clients, and followers to take action by directing them to your website, where they can learn more about your products and services, rate them, buy them, and submit feedback that is visible to your target market.

Digital marketing is inexpensive. Although some people pay for web advertisements, the cost is still less than traditional marketing. Data and results are simple to keep track of. You may monitor your campaigns at any moment using Google Analytics and the insights capabilities provided by most social media platforms. Unlike traditional marketing tactics, online marketing allows you to observe what is and is not working for your company in real time, allowing you to immediately change and improve your results. On an equal footing: With a great digital marketing strategy, any firm, regardless of size, can compete with any rival. Traditionally, a smaller business has struggled to match the elegance of its larger competitors' fixtures and fittings. A clean, well-thought-out website with a smooth client journey and excellent service is king online – not size. Real-time results: Unlike waiting for a fax or form to be returned, you won't have to wait weeks for a boost to your business. At the stroke of a button, you can observe the number of visits to your site and subscribers grow, as well as peak trade periods, conversion rates, and much more. Developing a Brand: A well-maintained website with relevant content that meets your target audience's needs and adds value can deliver tremendous value and lead creation prospects. Using social media channels and personalized email marketing in the same way. How often do your customers and prospects distribute your sales fliers around on the spot? Using social media share buttons on your website, email, and social media channels allows you to spread your message fast online.

When you consider that the average Facebook user has 190 friends, and only about 12% of those friends see their liked posts, your one message has reached 15 new people. Consider how many of them enjoy and spread your message, and how many of their friends do the same. This is why high-quality material is crucial. So, which type of marketing is more effective? On the following grounds, it is recommended to employ both traditional (physical) and digital marketing materials:

- The brain perceives physical material as more "real." It has a purpose and a location. Because it engages with its spatial memory networks, it is better connected to memory.

- Physical material involves more emotional processing, which is important for memory and brand associations.
- Physical materials produced more brain responses associated with internal feelings, implying that the ads are more "internalized."

## How can businesses combine digital and traditional marketing?

The organization's digital marketing initiatives must be supported by traditional marketing approaches. They don't work in isolation from one another. Only hard copy marketing materials, such as brochures to someone interested in the organization's services, can be utilized to strengthen a relationship with a contact, referral partner, or client. Rather of choosing an all-or-nothing approach, it appears that combining the advantages of paper with the convenience and accessibility of digital will yield the best results. A business communicates with a group of people about its products or services. Bidirectional communication is possible. Customers can also inquire about the company's products and services and give suggestions. Phone calls, letters, and emails are the most common modes of contact. Social media, chat, websites, and emails are the most common modes of communication.

Designing, developing, and releasing a campaign takes extra time. There is always a quick way to create an internet campaign and make changes as it progresses. Campaigning is easier with digital tools. It is done for a specific audience from the creation of campaign concepts to the sale of a product or service. The information is open to the broader public. Then, using search engine strategies, it is designed to reach the target audience. It is a traditional marketing strategy; best It's the most effective way to reach a worldwide audience. It's difficult to assess a campaign's effectiveness. Analytics makes it easy to assess a campaign's effectiveness.

Coca-simple Cola's yet brilliant 'share a coke' campaign has swept the nation this summer, allowing people to replace the coke brand name with their own and share the experience with others. This has to be one of the most groundbreaking marketing initiatives ever, demonstrating what can be accomplished when technology is properly integrated into the marketing mix. It's given digital marketers all across the world a successful case study to look to in the budget struggle against traditional types of marketing almost overnight. Since 2013, Coke has modified its marketing to mirror how people consume media, using a complimentary mix of online and offline media. Furthermore, digital is at the center of this campaign since it allows them to achieve their goal of offering "personalized brand experiences" and demonstrates what the future of marketing holds.

### CHAPTER 3

## TYPES OF DIGITAL MARKETING APPROACHES

### PULL AND PUSH DIGITAL MARKETING

Digital marketing is divided into two categories, one of which is pull digital marketing. It seeks to persuade people to come to you by visiting your business or making a call to action. Websites and other internet-based platforms are frequent instances of pull digital marketing. Inbound marketing is another term for pull marketing. Push digital marketing is another type of digital marketing. It pushes the marketing material directly to your customers. SMS, email, and RSS are common examples of personalized messages sent to customers. Outbound marketing is another term for push marketing.

# Importance of Digital Marketing

Digital marketing allows you to reach and engage target audiences in a variety of ways. They examine how a website may fulfill the criteria of marketing as a fundamental aspect of digital marketing.

- Identify needs from customer comments, enquiries, requests, and complaints submitted via the web site's email facility, bulletin boards, chat rooms, and, of course, sales patterns (seeing what's selling and what's not), and by observing new customer groupings identified through data mining of customer data, sales, and interests. Remember to use online surveys and direct from customer online feedback methods, such as those listed to gauge satisfaction and solicit suggestions for service or product changes. Finally, there are numerous online secondary research sources, many of which offer free in-depth insights into customer needs.

- Anticipate marketing. Don't put it off any longer. Email marketing can greatly boost your affiliate revenues.

The process of transporting products from the manufacturer to the intended user is referred to as location in the marketing mix. In other words, it's about how and where your product is purchased. This migration could be facilitated by a number of middlemen, including distributors, wholesalers, and retailers.

Building your shop in the wrong location reduces foot traffic, which means less sales. It's even worse if your shop is in the right location but you don't have any stock.

## How Does This Affect Digital Marketing?

All of these things are relevant to digital marketing. If the firm does not the various types of digital marketing platforms where businesses may advertise their brands and receive a high-quality response

## Different Digital Advertising Platforms

Select ad space in selected websites where you can receive good traffic based on your audience profile and your merchandise. From banner advertisements to movies, display ads may be anything. It is one of the most effective digital branding strategies in the online world. Create engaging movies or graphics that will speak for your brand instead of building text-based marketing. Take the time to follow your goals and carefully select the websites that your target audience frequents. Pay-per-click (PPC) When your visitors arrive, they will be asked to fill out certain forms.

## What Qualifies a Digital Marketer?

Beginning with the must-have hard talents and concluding with the traits that the very best

Digital Marketers earn over time—often in unrelated fields—the following list outlines the skills a top-tier Digital Marketer should have.

## Search engine optimization and search engine marketing

It doesn't matter how hard you work as a digital marketer if no one sees it! The first and possibly most important step in connecting with your audience is driving traffic to your web properties, particularly your landing pages. To be a successful Digital Marketer, you must be an expert at maximizing SEO and SEM.

### Analyze the data

While they don't need to be as skilled with data analytics as, say, a Data Scientist, they do need to be able to deal with it. Inbound marketing methods and strategies, as opposed to typical outbound strategies, are provided by an inbound marketing agency. Inbound marketing organizations work to position a company online so that customers can find them, gain trust over time, and eventually make sales. Inbound tactics can produce considerable returns over time, but they usually take longer (six months to a year or more) before leads and revenues "hockey stick."

## AGENCY FOR SEO

SEO (search engine optimization) services assist their clients' websites and content rank higher in search results. They will hire experts to do the following:

- Keyword investigation
- Audits of websites
- Audits of backlinks
- Content for websites and blogs
- Metadata evaluation (checking the quality of URL, title tags, meta descriptions, etc.)
- Optimization of video descriptions

## Listening and Participation

Unfortunately, social media marketers typically overlook this crucial area. This refers to what happens after the pieces have been written and published. It has to do with how you connect with your audience and how you engage them. This includes responding to messages and comments, creating interactive content, offering useful information, and, most importantly, listening to your audience in order to provide them with the most relevant content.

**Analytics**

You need to know what works and what doesn't when it comes to social media marketing tactics. This is where analytics can help. You can find data on almost anything using a variety of tools and techniques. These metrics are then utilized to tweak campaigns or confirm that something is working or not.

## Strategy & Consulting for a Full Digital Marketing Plan

To disseminate information and keep the project going forward, the marketing leader or outsourced marketing team must spend time evaluating analytics and data, establishing strategic plans, and meeting often with key stakeholders.

## Website Design for Growth

All sales and marketing efforts are coordinated through the website. You can't just set it and forget it. The example company will work on one web page per month to develop and enhance their site, either by building a new page or altering an existing page's design, copy, or function.

## Creating Leads (Release 1 landing page every other month)

During the sales process, prospective buyers want to educate themselves. The business will publish e-books.

## Requirements for a Successful Launch

A strategy is only as good as its execution. For successful implementation, there are three requirements:

1. A solid foundation You can't do social media if you don't have social media profiles, and you can't send emails if your list isn't up to snuff. Make sure you have everything you'll need to finish the job quickly and effectively.

2. Experts: No one individual can do everything. Finding someone who excels at everything: data analysis, strategic planning, project management, content writing, SEO, graphic design, email marketing, database administration, sales, and website design, development, and coding would be challenging, if not impossible. Make sure you have personnel who are informed and skilled to fill those positions.

3. Money and Time: To complete the task, the strategy requires technology, resources, and people. Is it worth it to spend money and effort on everything? I won't bother you with the ROI equation right now, but it's all mathematics when it comes down to it. How much do you have to sell in order to earn a profit on your investment?

## Marketing Budget Estimates

When it comes to money, you're definitely curious about the price of the sample plan. Most firms bill between $125 and $250 per hour. The estimated annual budget to complete everything on the list, including personnel, technology, and advertising, is $175K to $250K. Companies spend 7-11 percent of their overall sales on marketing on average. A corporation with $1.6 million in annual revenue should be able to afford such a comprehensive strategy.

## Strategies for Saving Money

1. Reduce your marketing efforts.

If your company is worth $500K, your investment level should be around $60,000. That means the digital marketing plan and budget example I provided before would be unattainable. However, if you're a tiny firm and can't afford to do all that marketing, there are some options. Reduce the quantity of blogs, emails, social media postings, and content offerings you send out, or perform less marketing in general. You can keep your schedule the same; it will just take longer to complete.

2. Include everyone in the process!

Alternatively, you can employ a professional to teach your internal team in a variety of activities and distribute the responsibility among a large number of individuals. Here are two of the most effective strategies to cut marketing expenditures while also improving customer service, but they both involve a cultural shift:

1. Everyone blogs: Teach as many employees as possible in your company to blog. You'll be able to write about the full customer experience, establish yourself as trusted industry thought leaders, and maintain a consistent stream of content from various perspectives. When customers or prospects have questions or require assistance, they will know where to go. And the more people who participate, the less work each individual has to perform.

2. Everyone goes social: Develop a company-wide social media plan. Define roles, duties, policies, and expectations with precision. As the saying goes, "many hands make light labor." It is not expected that everyone will be an adept blogger or social media master. A leader will still be required to oversee strategy and operations, manage projects, coach, teach, train, and

ensure value and quality control. It is easier and faster for marketers to constantly delivering good content to your target audience if people within the firm can offer their industry knowledge, skills, and insights.

## Conclusion

Your online store is similar to your physical store. It's a place where clients may "walk-in" and learn more about you and your products. The majority of your customers will find you there initially. It's also the only way for people to locate you if you don't have a real business! That's why having a digital presence that's easy to find, informative, valuable, and simple to use is critical. However, deciding where to spend your digital marketing money can be difficult. There are so many possibilities that it might be daunting. Take a step back to look at what you've done in the past, what's working and what isn't, and where you can improve to establish a realistic digital marketing plan and budget. Good data and analysis will ensure that you spend your money where it will yield the most return on investment for your company.

# CHAPTER 4

# TOP BRANDS' DIGITAL MARKETING TIPS AND TRICKS

here is no doubt that digital marketing is critical to the success of any firm, regardless of industry. So, what are some digital marketing best practices we can learn from larger (and better-funded) companies? Many businesses have realized the value of digital marketing in attracting new clients as a result of the pandemic. According to eMarketer, digital marketing will expand by 36% from 2020 to 2022, accounting for 54% of marketing budgets!

Why? Because digital marketing allows us to see what clients desire firsthand. With the rise of digital marketing data, tools, analytics, and software, it's much easier to see and adapt to actual online customer behavior. Businesses can now acquire valuable insights into their customers' brains thanks to digital marketing.

Digital marketing, when done correctly, may help your company target and reach its consumers, classify new ones, enhance revenue, and experience long-term success. These digital marketing strategies will increase your company's online visibility and link you with new customers.

**Top 10 digital marketing strategies you can utilize to develop your business**

1. **Use SEO and content marketing together.**

SEO is not a new concept. For a long time, SEO was primarily concerned with keywords and coding. Then Google became more intelligent. While SEO alone is ineffective, we determined that integrating SEO and Content Marketing is one of the most effective marketing strategies for 2022. The majority of the metrics used in Google's algorithm nowadays are related to content (as even Google admits) and the engagement gained through the spread of exceptional information. Using a variety of material formats (visual, text, video, infographics, audio, and so on) performs considerably better than using only one.

More content - As more organizations adopt content marketing, the competition is becoming more intense. Noise and information overload pervade everything you do online. Every firm must publish better and more content in order to succeed. According to HubSpot statistics, writing at least once a week is crucial for ROI, and when you write less frequently, your ROI declines dramatically. However, it is not a question of quantity against quality, but rather a perfect balance of both.

Content that is valuable should be interesting, educational, and sympathetic. Valuable content not only responds to the search intent or question posed by the search engine, but it is also structured to encourage involvement, such as email subscriptions, sharing, comments, and other behaviors that add to ROI.Original content — Content can be audio, video, or text, but whichever you choose, make sure it is good and original. You can hire an expert to develop content for your website and social media platforms if you are unable to create unique, captivating, and good material on your own. This is where a strong content marketing strategy will be required like never before. Knowing where a visitor is in the conversion process isn't always easy, but if you've done a good job coding content (applying tracking codes so you know what type of content drove them to your site) and use tools that let you track where visitors have been in the past, you can make an educated guess as to what content they require. You're more likely to convert visitors to purchasers if you give the correct material at the right moment. Reach is crucial. All other factors being equal, the better your ROI, the more people you bring to your site. One of the reasons it's critical to have many social networks and links on your content is so that people can simply share it.

## 2. Make Yourself Visible on Relevant Social Media Platforms

Being visible online is critical for any business's success, especially in today's environment where nearly all enterprises have gone digital. It's one method to set yourself out from the herd. As a result, you must establish an online presence on relevant social media networks. There are numerous social networks to choose from, but you must determine where your clients spend the most of their time and target them there. Choose those that are relevant to your company and prospects, and establish a presence there.

Also, unless your last name is Kardashian, social media is not the best location to promote your items. Sharing and engaging on social media is the goal. However, social networking is not the most effective digital marketing channel for demonstrating company development.

## 3. Make your website mobile-first friendly.

Your website and social media networks must be accessible on both desktops and mobile devices to ensure that your content is mobile friendly. Customers mostly access the internet via smartphones and tablets. As a result, making your website and content available to users on all screen sizes is critical. Use the latest color schemes and trends to update your website design.

## 4. Make Use of the Correct Tools

Digital marketing is a collection of methods directed towards a variety of channels, such as SEO, PPC, and social media. You'll need the correct digital marketing tools to run effective campaigns if you want to have an integrated marketing mix. You must also build competence in their use and application in the appropriate setting.

## 5. Be a Design Superstar

Much of what makes digital marketing successful is based on design. You need solid design skills whether you're designing a website, a landing page, or an image for your website, commercial, or infographic. When it comes to design, not everyone is a genius, but there are several tools that can help.

Canva - Canva is a fantastic tool for designing social media images, whether for your profile or for use in posts. Canva has some templates that assist you create great-looking images even if you have no idea about layout or which fonts work together. They're always introducing new photos and tools to help you out, such as infographic layouts. Photoshop is a fantastic design tool, despite its high price tag.

Fortunately, Adobe's whole creative cloud is now available for as little as $29 a month for students and a bit more for businesses. Photoshop used to be more difficult to use, but now there are numerous videos available on YouTube, and Photoshop now includes small instructions when you hover over the buttons.

## 6. Make a mailing list

Email is still a powerful driver of ROI in digital marketing. In fact, email generates a $36 return on investment for every dollar spent! But you must do it correctly. Make sure your website has a sign-up form for an email newsletter. Deliver useful material to your subscribers rather than just advertisements. Make up stories.

## 7. Invest in digital marketing

Now, many people are paying money on digital advertisements. Few can demonstrate any sort of return on investment. Google Ads, YouTube Ads, social media advertising on platforms like

Facebook, Instagram, LinkedIn, and Twitter, Snapchat, and Tiktok are all things you might test to achieve digital marketing success. We've tried everything. Contextual content promotion is one method we've discovered for bringing in relevant traffic, engaging users, and converting leads. We track down your target demographic on the internet and serve them an ad. But not a product advertisement. Also, promote your stuff.

The audience is then gathered into a retargeting pool. We bombarded them with offerings such as e-books, webinars, and free advice. This allows us to offer CPCs that are 80% lower than the industry average and CTRs that are 4-5 times higher.

## 8. Use infographics whenever possible.

People enjoy infographics because they are visually appealing. It's worth noting that our brains comprehend images much faster than words. People will exchange pictures more frequently than texts since a picture is worth a thousand words.

## 9. Keep an eye on your analytics.

Analytics is on the opposite end of the spectrum from creativity, but it's the exact combination you need for digital marketing success. Google Analytics is ideal for determining the most important aspects of your website and how users navigate there. If you want to learn how to utilize Google Analytics to gain insights, you can use the Google Data Studio to practice with data from Google's e-commerce site. A variety of excellent analytics solutions exist outside of Google Analytics. You can utilize individual metrics from each social network (e.g., Facebook, Pinterest, etc.), or you can use a dashboard application like Cognos (from IBM) to bring them all together, or you can pay for a more powerful tool to acquire more insights.

## 10.    Create cross-channel strategies and campaigns.

Integrating various approaches can be difficult, especially in a larger organization where separate teams manage multiple platforms or different ad agencies handle different areas of marketing, such as content marketing, paid advertising, and social media. However, you must integrate to attain meaningful digital marketing success.

## planning strategy

A strategic plan is the initial stage in integration. If you don't already have one, go here to learn how to make one. Coordination comes from strategic aspects like message, but even mission and goals can help integrate efforts by providing a framework under which teams can develop posts, infographics, and the metrics that are used to evaluate them.

## Creative brainstorming sessions

It is critical to bring everyone together. Everyone should have time to explain what they're working on and gain feedback from the group on how to expand a project across numerous platforms and creative endeavors. A style guide is essential. List the color palette, fonts, and approved variations in the style guide to ensure uniformity across your marketing activities (including traditional advertising). The style guide may include logos in various sizes and styles, photographs of the leadership team, and other graphic components.

## A comprehensive strategy

A single point person in charge of digital marketing success is essential for coordinating efforts across departments. Some companies have an approval process in which everything must be approved by the CEO before going live. I'm not a fan of this strategy since it slows down the process, and unlike traditional advertising, digital media is a fast-moving river where building a dam causes the flow to back up, allowing a lot of flotsam and jetsam to accumulate, which stinks and further clogs the pipeline. Using a digital master calendar or similar device, such as an app, to allow everyone to post what they're working on, the assets they plan to use, and when the creative endeavor will go live, is a preferable technique. But posting plans isn't enough; everyone should be obliged to check this master calendar every day to see how their ideas tie in with those currently in the works. Reusing a graphic generated by another team, for example, not only saves time and money, but also generates a visual that helps customers (and potential customers) correlate the two efforts–increasing frequency.

### It's your turn.

Digital marketing is essential for your business's success, and we hope that our list of tips will keep you on track. These strategies have been tried and true, and when used correctly, they can help you go ahead of the competition.

## Consumer Understanding

Who will most likely purchase the product, how frequently will they purchase it, what price will they pay, and where will they purchase it? Consumers have specific desires and requirements. Their earnings range from high to moderate to low. They can choose from thousands of products, ranging from high-end luxuries to everyday essentials. They have a diverse range of customs and tastes, from ethnic to generic goods. Every day, consumers have an impact on production decisions.

The final customers and users of items are known as consumers. Any company's goal is to create and sell a product. *The following is what the manager must do:*

- Create it in the format that customers prefer.
- Produce it when customers request it.
- Put it on the market where people want it.
- Sell it at a price that customers will pay.

*Managers must collect market data in order to make the following daily decisions:*

- What is the maximum quantity of a product that customers are willing to buy?
- Who makes these things and who competes for those customers?
- What are the prices that customers are willing to pay?
- What is the rate at which products and information move across the distribution channels?
- Should production be raised or decreased based on this information?

## Client feedback

People are given the opportunity to experience the product before being asked for their views. A first step would be to enlist the assistance of friends and neighbors, as well as to determine testing choices for the new product. It's critical to keep asking customers for feedback as the product sells. A marketing strategy should contain this step. Ask the following questions to your customers.

- How do they feel about the product and the company?
- Do they like it?
- Will they repurchase it?
- When will you know?

Continuous data should be acquired in each location about sales volume and changes in rivals, product life cycles, new products, vendor service, and competitors. Remember that generic data will yield general outcomes, whereas detailed data will allow for more detailed analysis and more accurate results. To optimize utility, each manager must choose what type of information is required and how much should be collected. The more information producers have about their clients, the more likely they are to satisfy them.

## Consumer purchase frequency

The frequency with which consumers make purchases is critical. The key to a successful outlet selection is repeat purchasing. When establishing manufacturing rate, shipping, and storage, marketing managers must consider how frequently consumers will purchase their items.

The following are the most prevalent purchasing patterns:

- **Daily** — Some products, such as milk, bread, and doughnuts, are purchased on a daily basis, requiring the maker to provide the product on a regular basis. These items are frequently perishable.

- **Weekly** — These are items with a shelf life of three to six weeks. Production inventory will need to be closely monitored for these products. Between deliveries, a producer must have the ability and capacity to hold products.

- **Monthly** — If a customer only buys one item per month rather than one per week, a larger consumer territory is required. Delivery will be less frequent, requiring more storage, either on the shelf or in the back room.

- **Seasonal** — These are items that are associated with a particular blooming season or holiday. These products are often only available for a limited time each year.

# CHAPTER 5

# WHAT IS CONSUMER BEHAVIOR

There's a lot more to marketing than coming up with a clever phrase or a song that people will hum for days. Consumer behavior is an important part of marketing. The study of how individuals make decisions about what they buy, desire, need, or do in relation to a product, service, or corporation is known as consumer behavior. Understanding consumer behavior is essential for predicting how potential customers would react to a new product or service.

It also assists businesses in identifying untapped prospects. Consumer eating habits have substantially boosted demand for gluten-free (GF) products, which is a recent example of a change in consumer behavior. Companies that kept track of customer eating habits developed gluten-free products to fill a need in the market. However, several companies failed to keep track of consumer behavior and were late to market with gluten-free products. Understanding consumer behavior allows proactive businesses to gain market share by anticipating shifts in consumer desires.

## The Three Elements

Understanding the three aspects that influence customer behavior: psychological, personal, and social, is critical to properly comprehending how consumer behavior affects marketing.

## Factors of Psychology

Many challenges that are unique to their mental process affect consumers in their daily lives. Psychological aspects can include a person's perception of a need or circumstance, their ability to learn or comprehend information, and their attitude. A person's perceptions and attitudes will determine how they respond to a marketing message. As a result, marketers must consider these psychological characteristics when developing ads to ensure that they appeal to their target demographic.

## Personal Aspects

Personal traits are characteristics that are unique to an individual and may not be shared by others in the same group. These qualities could include a person's decision-making process, unique habits and hobbies, and viewpoints. When it comes to personal characteristics, age, gender, background, culture, and other personal difficulties all play a role. An older individual, for example, is likely to have different consumer behaviors than a younger person, which means they will choose products differently and spend money on things that a younger generation may not be interested in.

## Social Aspects

Social traits are the third component that has a substantial impact on consumer behavior. Social influencers can range from a person's family to social contact, work or school communities, or any group of people with whom they associate. It can also refer to a person's socioeconomic status, which includes things like income, living conditions, and educational attainment. When designing marketing plans, social elements are complex and can be tough to analyze. However, social aspects in consumer behavior must be taken into account because they have a significant impact on how consumers respond to marketing messages and make purchasing decisions. Consider how a well-known spokesperson can affect purchasers.

## Models of Consumer Behavior

Several models, such as the black box, personal variables, and complicated models, have been established through research and observation to assist explain why customers make decisions.

The black-box concept is based on external stimulus-response, which means that something causes the consumer to make purchasing decisions impacted by a variety of factors such as marketing messages, sampling, product availability, promotions, and price. Consumers make decisions based on internal considerations when affected by the personal-variable model. Personal beliefs, belief systems, values, traditions, ambitions, and any other internal motivation are examples of internal factors. A digital ecosystem is a collection of linked information technology resources that can work together. Suppliers, customers, trading partners, applications, third-party data service providers, and all related technologies make up digital ecosystems. The ecosystem's success depends on interoperability.

Market share leaders commonly establish and dominate digital ecosystems; the approach has keiretsu roots and is rapidly impacting transformation in a variety of industries, including consumer goods, automobiles, and healthcare. An ecosystem helps an organization to control new and old technologies, establish automated processes around them, and constantly expand their business by integrating B2B practices, corporate applications, and data. An ecosystem's unmanaged organic growth can be catastrophic to a corporation. When constructing an ecosystem, it's critical to verify that all dependencies have been recognized and can be managed. A thriving ecosystem requires the creation of a digital ecosystem map. The digital ecosystem map is a visual representation of the organization's digital tools and platforms. It depicts processes, including how data is transmitted across ecosystem components and whether the process is automated or human. To be effective, mapping should also describe which systems are not currently connected or able to communicate and exchange data, as well as who the users of each system are and who is accountable for their upkeep.

## How do digital ecosystems function?

The technical, legal, and business challenges that digital ecosystems face are enormous. Some of the most significant problems are service orchestration, delivery, and monetization, as well as customer communication and data management (CCM and CDM, respectively) across the entire ecosystem.

*The following are the different types of ecosystem management tools:*

- research applications, such as data storage and visualization, resource libraries, and archives;
- engagement tools, such as email marketing, donor management tools, and customer relationship management (CRM) software;
- collaboration tools, such as email, file sharing, instant messaging, and video conferencing;
- public platforms, such as websites

# How do you construct a digital ecosystem map?

Any digital transformation requires a digital ecosystem map. The map's purpose is to clear what an organization has to work with, ensure that they have the right tools to support their objectives, and ensure that they are as efficient and successful as possible in attaining those objectives.

*The steps for creating a digital ecosystem map are as follows:*

1. Make a tool list first. Make a list of all the programs and systems in use within the company.
2. Keep track of who utilizes the tools. Determine who utilizes each system and app, as well as who is responsible for them. This ensures that the ecosystem includes all key players.
3. Sort out how each tool is used. Define what each system and app accomplishes, as well

as the departments and purposes for which they are used. Ownership and department should be used to categorize systems.

4. Create links between tools. Indicate whether data is transferred automatically or manually between tools and where it is transferred. Take note of which duties are being duplicated and which systems have similar features.

5. Determine how effective each tool is. Examine whether any tools are operating poorly and should be replaced, updated, or combined. The folks who utilize the tool on a daily basis should submit feedback.

6. Make each tool a priority. Determine the importance of each tool to the organization. Consider the importance of tools in terms of their immediate necessity for the organization when replacing or adding them, and design an order in which they should be implemented.

# Different kinds of digital ecosystems

The digitizer ecosystem, platform ecosystem, and super platform ecosystem are the three basic forms of digital ecosystems. Digitizer ecosystems are focused on digitizing an existing product with the support of business partners while keeping management complexity to a minimum. Digitizer ecosystems can enhance system functionality and generate revenue through digital services. This ecosystem typically consists of 20 to 100 established partners from five different industries.

Businesses with excellent product competencies, limited digital capabilities, and a predominantly internal emphasis will benefit from the digitizer ecosystem. It's ideal for companies that want to make their existing product smart and connected. An automotive company that collaborates to gain the technology and intellectual property (IP) needed to connect their cars with relevant digital services is an example of a digitizer ecosystem.

*Digitizer ecosystems are less advanced than platform ecosystems.*

They are focused on integrating users and smart devices on a platform smoothly while ensuring high service levels and minimizing impediments. Platform utilization generates revenue streams for the platform ecosystem. The ecosystem's data can be applied to similar enterprises and service models. Platform ecosystems typically include between 50 and 10 million partners spread across five industries. Companies with strong digital capabilities and a strong focus on external expertise benefit the most from the platform ecosystem. Established tech startups and companies are more likely than nontech enterprises to adopt this platform as their primary business strategy. Xiaomi, a Chinese electronics business that develops and invests in a number of product kinds, including smartphones, laptops, fitness brands, and mobile apps, is an example of a platform ecosystem. Xiaomi collaborates closely with its contributors, the device manufacturers, to create a smart home platform that includes a wide range of smart, connected gadgets.

The most complicated type of digital ecosystem is the super platform ecosystem. They concentrate on combining many platforms into a single integrated solution while also obtaining user data from that platform. This type of ecosystem provides a diverse set of user data while also converting the data into money through complementary business models. In most cases, the super platform ecosystem comprises at least 10 million partners from at least ten different businesses. Companies with significant digital capabilities and an established platform from the start, as well as a desire to collaborate with external partners, are most suited for super platform ecosystems. As a result, well-established tech enterprises favor this environment. A virtual assistant that combines shopping, payment, transportation, and communication services into one user-friendly option is an example of a super platform ecosystem.

Many businesses discover that combining multiple ecosystems yields the best results. Amazon Alexa, for example, makes use of all three. A digitizer ecosystem is used to upgrade the smart speaker's hardware and voice recognition functionality; a platform ecosystem is used to add skills and applications to expand Alexa's services; and a super platform ecosystem is used to connect all other platforms.

## What are the benefits of digital ecosystems?

Many companies' strategies have recently included digital transformation. No matter where a firm is on its digital path, establishing a digital ecosystem to boost performance and assist with connections outside the company is critical. By removing any difficulties associated with outmoded, traditional B2B services, the digital ecosystem allows a firm to focus its energy on facilitating commercial value. In addition, digital ecosystems increase the value of by assisting businesses in reliably meeting service-level agreements (SLAs), providing speedy solutions, and swiftly surfacing expectations.

Supply chains are likewise being transformed by digital ecosystems. Supplier ecosystems are the result of supply chains that previously operated in distinct marketplaces coming together in digital ecosystems to assist the development of new products and services. Although most businesses still rely on the old supply chain, the emerging paradigm of digital ecosystems is altering the business world by building linear connections between suppliers and customers, opening up new business prospects.

## The advantages of digital ecosystems

*The following are some of the advantages of a digital ecosystem:*

- Technology adoption is more rapid. Companies can now integrate new technology in previously unmanageable and complicated ways, allowing them to fully utilize cloud and SaaS services.
- Creation of new revenue streams. Ecosystem integration generates new revenue streams while also allowing businesses to track and analyze a wide range of data. They can utilize this information to develop new, more valuable products and services.
- Lower costs due to improved business processes. The construction of a digital ecosystem and digital transformation boost workflow efficiency and customer and partner interactions. Operational costs are also reduced by automated data

procedures and greater business wide efficiency.

## Best practices in the digital ecosystem

It is critical for enterprises to be open to change when developing an integrated digital ecosystem. Using contemporary technologies, digital transformation focuses on rewriting an organization's goods, processes, and strengths. This restructuring will not be possible unless the organization is willing to accept all of the prospective changes.

*The following are some other recommended best practices for creating and maintaining a robust and productive digital ecosystem:*

Reconsidering the business concept Business processes, management styles, silos, contracts, and governance structures should all be examined to see if they are still relevant in the digital age.

- Promoting a collaborative and open culture. Strong communication and collaboration between enterprises are essential for a well-rounded, effective digital ecosystem.

- Bringing together a huge number of various partners. Other industries' expertise is needed in digital ecosystems. As a result, the stronger and more productive an ecosystem is, the more partners it has and the more industries from which they come. The typical ecosystem has 27 partners, whereas the most successful ecosystems have roughly 40.

- Develop a large user base. Market share leaders — companies with the biggest profit margin in their specialized market — typically establish and operate the most effective digital ecosystems because they are best positioned to attract partners with the requisite skills and financing.

- Establish a global presence. A digital ecosystem's geographic reach is another indicator of its success. It is beneficial to work across a variety of geographic, language, and cultural boundaries, just as it is necessary to gather a wide number of partners. Successful digital ecosystems cover ten or more nations, while average ecosystems have partners in five places.
- Keep up with technological advancements. Sharing and, as a result, creativity will be hampered by outdated software, failed connections, and cumbersome data centers. The most successful digital ecosystems invest in the most cutting-edge and best-in-class technologies, as well as people who are passionate about learning about new digital capabilities.

# CHAPTER 6

# AUDITS OF DIGITAL ECOSYSTEMS

While digital ecosystems might improve corporate processes and efficiency, they can also deplete productivity, capital, and morale. If the systems in an ecosystem don't communicate or require a lot of human updating in order for reports to be relevant, the company is wasting time and money on things that aren't helping it develop. Ecosystem audits are the most effective technique to ensure ecosystem health.

*The following are the most important questions to address during an audit:*

- What are the tools' management procedures? Is there a governance model in place to support the tools? Is there a future plan or the ability to respond to needs as they arise?

- How do the present tools help the organization achieve its vision and objectives? Is the brand experience and personality consistent throughout the tools?

- How does knowledge circulate throughout the company? How might the digital ecosystem help the organization's operations and workflows run more smoothly?
- How do people within the ecosystem collaborate? Who has access to what information? What can people do to improve their efficiency and effectiveness?

Answering these questions and doing a comprehensive digital ecosystem audit may take a long time, but it will provide you a better understanding of how your company's digital environment operates. The company can then use this to save money and grow.

## Management of Digital Ecosystems

In response to digital transformation and the integration of digital ecosystems, a new discipline called Digital Ecosystem Management (DEM) has evolved for enterprises. The goal of Digital Ecosystem Management is to harness the ecosystem to expand a firm by leveraging other people's creativity and all other available resources.

## Digital ecosystems examples

A digital ecosystem is an example of a modern banking application. These apps establish ecosystems that bring together all services and applications, such as expenditure managers, digital wallets, online banking, and digital passbooks, in one place. Danske Bank, a Danish company, developed an online system that combines customer information with real estate listings. Potential homebuyers received tax, electric, and heating cost estimates, as well as a directory of realtors, information, and service providers, as well as sound, dependable financial guidance.

Digital ecosystems have also proven effective in the healthcare industry. Every touchpoint in a patient's journey is included in a digital healthcare ecosystem, including arranging visits, receiving appointment reminders, storing test results, and tracking prescriptions. The ecosystems assist healthcare organizations in meeting industry and government requirements by ensuring that they have the necessary documentation and auditing capabilities to meet mandates such as the Health Information Exchange (HIE), the Health Insurance Portability and Accountability Act (HIPAA), and the Health Information Technology for Economic and Clinical Health Act (HITECH).

Many healthcare businesses are looking at incorporating artificial intelligence (AI) and machine learning (ML) into their systems to improve consumer experiences and decision-making processes. A digital ecosystem will enable this by ensuring that the right data is available at the right time, allowing healthcare businesses to fully benefit from AI and machine learning. Digital ecosystems are also being adopted by the automotive industry. To obtain the essential parts in the past, vehicle manufacturers either forged an association with an original equipment manufacturer or built contractual connections with hundreds of suppliers. A typical automaker now manufactures autonomous, electric cars that are connected to the company's digital platform using a network of more than 30 partners, five different industries, and multiple nations.

## Designing Data Protection Barriers and Pathways

### 1. Lack of a Model or Process

Person explained that switching to a new digital marketing system (CMS, email, automation, personalization, analytics, and so on) is not easy. "There's a lot more to it than simply IT," he added. Businesses rely on digital marketing to generate a substantial percentage of their revenue, so using less-than-best methods could jeopardize revenue and careers. According to Person, clear and proven processes are required in marketing and IT.

"When implementing a new digital marketing system, it's vital that marketing uses cutting-edge best practices," he noted. "They can't just market in the same way they always have."

***To achieve maximum marketing impact with little resources, digital marketers should:***

- Map content to personas and lifecycles.
- Perform a data analysis to identify significant visitor segments
- Use A/B multivariate testing to enhance response
- Use basic rules-based customization to identify locations that get the most return

"Marketers' transition to cross-channel digital marketing is similar to manufacturing's transition to ERP systems in the 1990s," Person added. "It was a difficult transition, but those producers who were successful leapfrogged their competitors." The new cross-channel digital marketing systems are what ERP was to manufacturing in terms of marketing. If you stick to a tried-and-true approach, you'll be a step ahead of your competition. You're in for a terrible experience if you use the wrong techniques."

## 2. Budget Restriction

Marketers should start with corporate objectives when thinking about "budgets." "Show how marketing objectives will help the company reach its goals," Person added. "After that, they must demonstrate how the digital approach will affect the marketing goals." It's the equivalent of drawing a cause-and-effect diagram. You have to put the pieces together." Demonstrate how digital marketing benefits the executive's bottom line, then create a business case or sensitivity analysis to demonstrate how a 5% to 20% increase in web conversions affects the company's bottom line.

Remember that if you buy simply a CMS to save money, you may wind up with higher expenses and risks as you piece together a system from other vendors. "An alternative is to purchase an integrated solution up front, in which all of the digital marketing parts are built to operate together," Person explained. "They may build an integrated system by adding new features as they need them, such as marketing automation, without having to worry about technical integration." "Digital strategists and digital marketing analysts are two of the most challenging skills to find, according to Person. "People with these skills should be brought in to help plan and create the new system."

### 3. Under Pressure for Quick Profits

There aren't enough people? No money to hire someone? That's something we've also heard. "We see a lot of firms that have pushed their in-house systems or single-purpose CMS to the limit," Person added. "Maintenance takes longer than new marketing campaigns." They're running as fast as they can, but they're not gaining enough traction to switch to a new system, either in terms of people or budget."

- Demonstrate to executives that falling behind the competition is a significant possibility. According to Site core's assessment of more than 800 enterprises, 84 percent of businesses are in the first two stages of digital marketing. "However, every industry has one top-level organization," he explained. "Brands, loyalty, and consumer minds are all on the rise. Consider Amazon vs. Barnes & Noble or Netflix vs. Blockbuster if you are slow to implement the new digital strategy."

- Demonstrate how marketing has a direct impact on company goals. Hire a process consultant if you don't know how to do this.
- Create a business case or sensitivity analysis that demonstrates the impact on corporate goals.
- When integrating the IT and new digital marketing strategy, stick to tried and true procedures.
- Enhance their employees' abilities

**4. Insufficient Resources**

The major things missing in this space, according to Person, are people skills. Every CMO and digital strategist I spoke with said they couldn't locate enough qualified employees or secure enough funding. He claims that digital strategists and marketing analysts are the most difficult to come by. "Marketers can no longer be 'Mad Men,' with all due respect to the excellent ladies I work with." Person stated, "They must become 'Math Men.'" "They must make decisions based on data." Instinct-driven marketing is fantastic for innovation, but it must be put to the test with data to determine which answer is the best."

"Digital strategists are hard to come by," added Person. "There simply aren't enough of us with both technical and marketing brains around." Organizations moving away from silo-channel marketing require the services of a digital strategist (DS). To put together a technological and marketing strategy, a DS is required. What channel portfolio balance best satisfies the intended audience? What technological and HR abilities are required to make this a reality? "How are we going to establish our performance with analytics?"

## 5. Change Management:

Person stated that implementing anything new is difficult. He continued, "Most of the move to cross-channel digital strategy (customer experience) is an organizational adjustment." "A wise CMO will engage an organizational development (OD) expert on how to implement and train individuals for their new duties. Some abilities will remain the same, but as you advance in your job, you'll require a greater range of expertise." A skills/HR implementation and training plan are required in addition to IT project management, according to Person.

**_Companies looking for a change should consider the three types below:_**

- The Burning Platform: "We must reform now or perish!" This has a high failure probability, according to Person, but it works quickly in a specific sort of organization and in a crisis.

"We can let everyone change gradually and eventually we'll get there without too much suffering," says Boil the Frog. This could work, but it might be too late for your company, according to Person.

- Train as a trapeze artist: "Make the new platform more secure and enjoyable." Provide extensive training and assistance. "Then set fire to the old platform." As an independent consultant, he used this strategy to help businesses migrate to Windows.

## What are the market entry barriers?

A barrier to market entry is a stumbling block (typically high expenses) to a product's success in a new market. Natural (i.e., due to the nature of the product and the characteristics of its target market) or artificial hurdles can be encountered (i.e., imposed by existing dominant players or governments to prevent newcomers and competition). Between a monopoly (where entry is nearly impossible) and a zero-cost market, the difficulty of entering a market lies (where everyone can enter without facing any obstacles). While monopolies are not uncommon, there is no such thing as a market with no costs. Normally, entering a market necessitates a financial investment (even if only in time). Because of the nature of the product or the industry it wants to join (e.g., high R&D expenses, owning or controlling a resource, the size of the network of existing customers), this expenditure can be large. These are called natural barriers to entering a market.

Those that do make such investments, on the other hand, have a natural incentive to discourage others from entering a market—in order to limit competition and so maximize profit. As a result, they may use aggressive pricing techniques, advertising and image-making, predatory acquisitions, litigation, loyalty schemes, high switching costs, or lobbying for government backing to construct artificial barriers. Special tax incentives for existing organizations can function as a barrier for newbie entities in terms of government support. Natural and artificial entry barriers can lead to monopolistic or oligopolistic situations in a market. In a free society, such as a liberal democracy, governmental action is required to maintain competition in that field. As a result,

# CHAPTER 7

# WHAT ARE THE ENTRY BARRIERS?

Barriers to entry are impediments or hindrances that prohibit a potential entrant seller from joining the market and competing with current competitors, such as high costs, government rules, patents, or other challenges. Barriers to entry represent a serious threat to the competitive scene since the playing field is not level, and new entrants have a difficult time catching up to established players.

For example, an established corporation with millions of clients may benefit from economies of scale and, as a result, price its goods extremely low. For a business that can't afford to offer at such a low price, this competitive advantage could be a genuine barrier to entry.

## Types of Entry Barriers

In today's market, there are three types of entry obstacles. There are three types of entry obstacles: natural barriers, artificial barriers, and government barriers.

## 1. Natural Entry Barriers

Natural barriers to entrance, also known as structural obstacles to entry, occur when the dynamics of an industry develop and the company's intrinsic position in the market. Among them are: Scale-Up Economies Economies of scale refer to a proportionate reduction in the cost of commodities due to a higher level of production. Many current players who serve the bulk of client's profit from cheap production costs, which allows them to lower the product's final price. This is a significant disadvantage for newcomers because they are unable to offer things at the prices set by these players.

## The Networking Effect

The network effect, also known as network externality or demand-side economies of scale, asserts that as more people use a commodity or service, it becomes more value. When compared to other IM apps, Whatsapp is more important to its users because most of their friends use it. They will be hesitant to switch to another IM app because Whatsapp performs the job for him. One of the key reasons why even Google is failing to penetrate the social media networking business is the network effect.

**High Prices**

Some sectors need new entrants to spend a significant amount of money on research and development and/or startup costs. These expenses include things like distribution, marketing, and production. There are also occasions where such high expenses result in break-even after a long period of time (like in the case of Uber and other aggregator businesses). Many new entrants are unprepared for such high prices and opt out of the market.

**Distribution Channels Access**

At times, one or a few enterprises have complete control over all distribution channels. This creates a barrier to entry for other businesses, as no company wants to see its competitor succeed.

Inelastic Demand Inelastic demand is defined as demand that is unaffected by price changes. When demand is inelastic, it becomes extremely difficult for new entrants to establish a place in the market. Ownership or Access to Raw Materials

There are occasions when the older players have exclusive access to or control over rare resources. For new enterprises, this creates a significant barrier to entry.

## 2. Artificial Entry Barriers

Artificial obstacles to entry, also known as strategic barriers to entry, are erected by current firms to prevent newcomers from entering the market. Among them are:

Pricing Techniques

There are roughly ten different pricing methods in use in the market, and each one, when implemented correctly, functions as a substantial barrier to entry for others. Big businesses, on the other hand, frequently employ predatory pricing strategies (also known as below-cost pricing) to minimize competition and close the market to newcomers.

**Marketing Techniques**

Many companies invest a lot of money to promote their product as the finest (or only) option on the market. As a result, a strong brand position is established in the market, which serves as a formidable barrier to overcome.

People start adopting many brand names as generic phrases because the marketing methods are so skillfully performed. For example, Jacuzzi is a brand, not a product.

**[Dis]advantages of technology**

There are occasions when the market leader and current companies enjoy a technological advantage over the competition. They are tight-lipped about their procedures and where they obtained the technology. Brand and Brand Loyalty Customers that are hesitant to test new brands develop brand loyalty as a result of strong marketing efforts.

## Customers' Switching Costs

The monetary and non-monetary costs that consumers experience as a result of changing product brands or suppliers are referred to as switching costs. Although monetary switching costs account for the majority of switching costs, there are also psychological, effort, and time-based switching costs that function as a barrier to consumers accepting new entrants.

## Patents and other legal constraints

Some pioneer businesses file patent applications for their concepts and technologies, making it impossible for other companies to enter the market and offer similar products. Crocs is an example of a company that has used patents to gain market share.

### 3. Government Entrance Barriers

The most difficult industries to break into are those that are extensively regulated by the government. Defence contractors, airlines, and railways are among these industries. Furthermore, the government may erect import or export restrictions, making it extremely difficult for international companies to enter or exit the local market.It may also require enterprises to get licenses before they begin operations, or the government may declare raw material access to be restr icted. The government may also provide subsidiaries to particular businesses, making it difficult for others to compete.

Examples of Entry Barriers

## Google

Google has carved itself such a stronghold on the internet that users and publishers alike see it as the most reliable search engine. Baidu, which benefited from the Chinese government's decision to prohibit Google, is the only company that has ever been able to exceed Google (in a country).

## Facebook

Facebook took advantage of the network effect. It developed a simple platform for connecting with friends from all across the world. There's no reason for a person to use any other social media network now that all of his friends are on Facebook.

## Uber

Uber shook up the taxi industry with a brilliant idea, massive finance, and predatory pricing. It initially benefited both customers and taxi drivers (partners), and both developed strong brand loyalty. People choose to utilize uber now that the predatory pricing model is no longer in effect, because they have grown loyal to the brand.

## What is programmatic marketing?

Many people refer to programmatic advertising as the "blackbox" of online marketing, full of jargon and growing at an almost exponential rate. It's a difficult issue to comprehend. So, what exactly is programmatic marketing? In its most basic form, programmatic advertising is the automated purchase and sale of web advertising. It's the process of selling inventory on publishing sites via various platforms, as well as buying inventory and placing adverts on a publisher's site. Programmatic marketing is another name for this type of marketing. Requests for proposals (RFPs), human negotiations, and manual insertion orders were all part of the process previously. The entire transaction now takes milliseconds from start to finish and involves multiple platforms.

## What is the process of programmatic advertising?

You've probably heard of programmatic advertising, also known as programmatic display ads, if you're a digital marketer. You may have even read articles about how programmatic advertising might help your brand's ad performance. However, we don't blame you if you don't fully comprehend the programmed procedure.

## Step-By-Step Explanation to the Most Common Programmatic Format

*Step 1:* When a user visits a website that employs programmatic advertising, the automated bidding process for serving an ad to that user begins.

*Step 2:* On their supply-side platform, the publisher lists the ad space for this viewer (SSP).

The SSP functions as the publisher's seller, informing advertisers of the site's, user's, and ad space attributes so that DSPs can place their bids. They essentially market the product (ad space) for sale.

**Step 3:** After receiving the ad space information, the SSP examines the user's cookies to discover elements such as their location, demographics, and interests.

**Step 4:** The appropriate demand-side platform (DSP) examines the user information provided by the SSP. DSPs help marketers find ad space that fits their budget and targeting criteria. It assigns a value to the ad placement based on the website and the characteristics of the user.

**Step 5:** The DSP bids for the ad placement on behalf of the advertiser. All of this occurs in real time, which is why programmatic advertising is also known as real-time bidding (RTB).

**Step 6:** Once the SSP has received all of the proposals, the SSP will choose the winner. There are several bid tactics available for various SSPs. Waterfall bidding, client-side bidding, and header bidding are the three types of bidding, with header bidding being the most efficient and equitable.

**Step 7:** After the winning offer is chosen, the SSP shows the user the ad on the publisher's site. The entire process of choosing a programmatic display ad takes milliseconds, all while the user's page loads.

## Most compelling reasons to adopt programmatic advertising

Here are five compelling reasons to make your advertising programmatic.

1. Make good use of your advertising budget. You may target users on a granular level with programmatic display advertising. You can target viewers with the appropriate

message, in the right location, at the right time if you have access to massive amounts of data (GDPR compliant, of course). This implies you're making better use of your advertising budget by avoiding wasting money on visitors who aren't likely to be interested in your goods.

2. Measurement and optimization in real time

Each ad's performance is tracked in real time with programmatic advertising. Advertisers no longer have to wait weeks for an excel sheet from their media agency, which is too late to optimize a live campaign. Advertisers may alter and optimize advertising in real time to test and enhance outcomes, as well as have complete control over their ad budget.

3. A method of purchasing media that is transparent.

Before programmatic advertising, firms had to rely on agencies and third parties to manage their advertising budgets. Brands can now have complete transparency regarding fees. Also, where and how much of their money is spent on which items.

## 4. It's not just about the numbers

Of course, knowing everything about a person isn't required for programmatic advertising targeting. Contextual targeting allows you to contact your target audience in a more natural – and less intrusive – approach. This allows you to target users based on keywords and a page's contextual significance.

## 5. Reach through multiple channels and formats

Your advertising should keep up with your ordinary user's growing number of digital touchpoints. Programmatic advertising is leading the charge in this area. It enables you to reach audiences across a variety of devices, including mobile, desktop, tablet, in-app, TV, and even out-of-home. The options are limitless!

Programmatic advertising currently encompasses a wide range of ad forms. It was mostly display advertising a decade ago, but now there are a variety of varied and rising possibilities.

## Display

Display is the most traditional kind of programmatic advertising. Instead of remaining static, advertising have become dynamic! New opportunities have emerged as a result of constant technical advancements, mobile optimization, and better data use. Many marketers have embraced programmatic creative techniques that target viewers with the right offer at the right moment, thanks to the advancement of new technologies.

## Video

Programmatically buying and serving digital video across platforms is now a major tactic for marketers. In 2019, programmatic video ad spending is expected to reach $13.4 billion, accounting for 76.5 percent of all digital video spending. Instream and out stream video are the two types of programmable video (with in-banner video sometimes classified as a type of outstream ad). More information on digital video can be found here.

## Indigenous and social

These are programmatic advertising that mix in with the content on a website, social media platform, or other app. Setting up contextual targeting as well as personalizing your adverts is critical, for example, for sponsored content.

Furthermore, DSPs now allow advertisers to buy programmatically across the major social ad networks, with social video being especially popular.

## Voice

The proliferation of streaming apps like Spotify, as well as Amazon's Alexa, has seen the emergence (or reemergence) of another format: voice. This format provides a wealth of contextual and user-specific targeting options. It's also evolving swiftly, with Google's DSP now allowing marketers to purchase programmatic audio advertisements.

## Out-of-home digital (DOOH)

With the proliferation of digital signs, programmatic is making its way into the world of out-of-home advertising. The arduous manufacturing process involving the advertiser, agency, media seller, and printer is on its way out. Integration across existing programmatic platforms, in its stead, allows for real-time DOOH and optimization and reactivity.

## Television

The amount of money spent on programmatic television advertising is currently insignificant (in the US it accounts for just 2.5 percent of total ad spend). Nonetheless, many major industry participants, like as Google, SKY, and Netflix, are laying the groundwork for the transition to programmatic TV. However, the format is the least developed of the programmable formats described.

## How do you make automated purchases?

Before you start buying programmatically, be sure you ask the proper questions and have a plan in place for what you want to accomplish.

*The following are the three major questions you should ask yourself:*

1. Can it assist us in reaching our intended audience?
2. Should we utilize programmatic advertising to raise brand awareness or to increase conversions?
3. How can programmatic advertising help me increase my revenue?

Once you have the answers to these questions, it will be much easier to figure out what should be your top priorities in terms of money and ad placements for your programmatic advertising plan. Of course, once you've decided on a plan, you'll need to choose the proper DSP for your business. There are a lot different providers out there, so be sure you're asking your DSP the proper questions.

**The most important aspects to consider while selecting a DSP**

1. Think about who you want to reach out to first. Which DSP has the best reach, segmentation, and channels for your target demographic? Remember that in some countries, SSPs are better than others, so choose the DSP that best fits your markets. Also, keep an eye on which publishers your DSP partners with in each target market.

2. How is your DSP billing you? Is it based on cost per thousand (CPM) or cost per click (CPC)? DSPs that charge by the CPM are

usually more open about their profit margins.

3. What kind of support services does your DSP offer? You might prefer a DSP with an agency-style setup, where you can get the help you need with campaign launch and optimization.

4.  Determine whether your DSP can execute a successful cross-channel plan if you so wish.

5. Think about how a DSP can work with the data management platform (DMP) or creative management platform you've chosen (CMP). Integration flexibility is more likely with smaller DSPs.

6.  At the end of the day, as Banner Flow Product Owner Jared Lekkas puts it, "you get what you pay for." Investigate your requirements for targeting, optimization, and control. If you want quality, be

prepared to pay for it! (If the price is too cheap, expect hidden fees.)

Your programmatic advertising campaigns will function in the same way as any other digital marketing campaign if you have the correct plan and technology in place. Make sure to try out different messaging and creatives, as well as different personas and locations and bid methods.

### *What is the best way to make programmatic display advertising?*

In general, marketers can create programmatic display advertising in one of two ways. It can be summarized as follows: with or without a creative management platform (CMP).

**With no CMP,**

Manually designing and then coding display advertising is absolutely possible. There are numerous tutorials and templates available online that will show you how to do this. The procedure, however, is incredibly slow. It also means you'll need people who are fluent in HTML5 and CSS, as well as having design expertise!

Furthermore, this procedure is monotonous, difficult to scale, includes too many manual activities, too many stakeholders, and takes much too long. For modern programmatic advertising, it is simply unworkable.

**Using a CMP**

You might also utilize a creative management tool like Bannerflow. CMPs handle all coding and allow for mass production of dynamic display advertising in a timely manner. CMPs also save time, deliver better advertising, and are preferred by marketing teams working on large-scale, data-driven display campaigns with artistic ambition.

## The advantages of a CMP

A creative management platform, in reality, cuts the time it takes to design, scale, and publish a programmatic display campaign in half. It allows for quick campaign A/B testing as well as real-time tuning and control of published advertising.

Furthermore, CMPs place a strong emphasis on design in display ad production. Plus, a CMP like Bannerflow is linked with all of the major programmatic networks, making it straightforward to publish to your preferred network.

**What does the future hold for programmatic advertising?**

Although programmatic advertising is not new, it is constantly evolving. This is a fascinating aspect of digital marketing because of new technologies, laws, and best practices. But what should you expect from programmatic in the future?

The fight over privacy continues: personal data and how advertisers can use it. GDPR, which set restrictions on the use of third-party data and how advertisers might use personal data for targeting purposes, altered the European marketing business in 2018. privacy will have a significant impact in 2020 and beyond. Indeed, the planned GDPR expansion will most likely broaden the scope of government limitations on the use of cookies in particular. More information can be found here.

**Tracking without cookies**

Cookies are becoming less and less useful for targeting as a result of rising issues with tracking imposed by various browsers. Expect to see deterministic and probabilistic tracking become more popular. More information on the two ways may be found here. The impact of artificial intelligence on media buying and programmatic creative in programmatic advertising, artificial intelligence has a variety of applications. With the rise of dynamic creative optimization, we're already witnessing a huge impact on customization and creative optimization (DCO).

Furthermore, IBM Watson has demonstrated that AI technology may significantly cut CPC.

## Programmatic advertising in-house

The Bannerflow/Digi day State of In-housing analysis found that advertising technology was the primary cause for 96% of respondents moving in-house. Brands taking control of their programmatic ad production and buying comes as no surprise in an age when transparency in digital marketing is a top priority. Programmatic advertising is always changing, therefore staying up to date on the latest technologies and methods is essential for a successful programmatic campaign. The Glossary of Programmatic Display Advertising A publisher is a company that sells digital media. Facebook, Schibsted, the New York Times, and Sanoma are some examples. Publishers can sell their inventory using a supply-side platform (SSP). One interface provides access to a multitude of networks, exchanges, and platforms. DSP (demand-side platform): An interface for purchasing advertising inventory. They can use a variety of SSPs or ad exchanges. In real-time auctions, algorithms are used to analyze bid requests and respond with bids and creatives. Ad tags are used by marketers to guide the browser to a specific ad. Each individual ad's size, type, and URL are determined. Additionally, ad tags collect campaign data and validate metrics like impressions and clicks. Ad server: Combines all campaign data (reporting, audience) from publishers, ad networks, search, social, and other sources. They also check to see if the impressions were served correctly and assist with creative optimization. Advertisers and affiliate marketers are connected through an affiliate network. Affiliates are compensated when an advertisement on their site effectively converts a visitor. Ad network: A company that acts as a middleman between publishers and advertisers. It collects unsold inventory from publishers and sells impressions at a discount (usually lower quality).

# CHAPTER 8

# WHAT PROGRAMMING CREATIVITY?

The automation of the building, publishing, and optimizing processes of display advertising is known as programmatic creative. It's a catch-all word for a variety of dynamic methods and technologies aimed at improving display ads' pace, scalability, relevance, and performance. The introduction and proliferation of a variety of programmatic advertising technology has also resulted in programmatic creative. The automated purchasing and selling of online advertising is known as programmatic advertising.

## Benefits of using programmatic creative?

The majority of display advertising is now supplied through programmatic advertising. A marketer is exceedingly unlikely to purchase goods programmatically. As a result, it is the standard means of displaying display advertising. Indeed, programmatic advertising is expected to account for 84.9 percent of all display advertising in the United States in 2019. It is predicted that by 2021, it would account for 88 percent of all US display advertising, with spending exceeding $81 billion! Marketers can take advantage of this increase by utilizing programmatic creative solutions such as creative management platforms (CMPs). Marketers can improve their display advertising success by integrating ad automation, data, and innovation.

## What is the significance of the "creative" component of programmatic creative?

If done correctly, programmatic creativity can help advertisers stand out in an increasingly crowded sector. This is especially crucial as more marketers turn to programmatic display and the barrier to entry continues to fall. But why is the "creative" component of programmatic creativity so crucial? To begin with, "creativity" in programmatic creative does not only refer to design! Marketers use programmatic buying to target (and retarget) consumers in this way. Data can be used creatively to reach the right customer at the right time with the appropriate message, as any media buyer will tell you.

Second, marketers must realize that behind every advertisement is a real person. Having the right message at the right moment is no longer enough to have an effect.

### What are the most important creative technologies for programmatic programming?

When programmatic creative and programmatic buying are combined, marketers can reach the right customer at the right time with the most relevant message. The examination of data from these procedures enables customized messaging to provide even more relevancy. As a result, marketing teams can boost performance by customizing ads. Many marketing teams now use programmatic customization as a standard practice. "Vast volumes of data mean[s] that advertising creative may dynamically change to be more relevant to customers, with ads changing to aspects like location, device, weather, time, and demographics," writes Nikki Gilliland of Consultancy. But how should this be accomplished?

## The three most important programmatic creative technologies

### Platforms for creative management (CMPs)

Marketing teams can use creative management solutions to quickly create and deliver high-quality programmatic display advertising across many media. Also, based on real-time ad analytics, use data to personalize pictures and messages. Even the tiniest in-house staff can become an ad factory with the help of a CMP. Teams can create endless display ad variations for multi-market, multi-audience campaigns thanks to smart automation. Meliá Hotels International, for example, uses the Bannerflow CMP to create approximately 2000 ad variations for different audience segments every week. This component of programmed creative creativity is impossible without a CMP. Furthermore, without a CMP, other programmatic creative technologies like dynamic creative and dynamic creative optimization (DCO) are too difficult or impossible to implement. This is because both need intricate HTML5 coding and time-consuming design processes, which a CMP can handle automatically.

## creative energy

Dynamic creative is becoming more popular and sophisticated. This is due to the ad tech infrastructure that has been developed to support programmatic advertising buying. This part of programmatic creativity has grown as a result of improved audience data, segmentation and targeting tactics, and optimized bidding strategies based on analytics. Dynamic creative is a programmatic creative strategy that selects the optimal pre-built display ad variation to deliver to a customer based on their location, what they're reading, the weather, and what device they're on, among other factors. It also refers to the usage of data feeds within a display ad to give the most current or relevant information for a specific viewer. For example, a UK-based sports betting company can retarget a German consumer with the latest odds and ad creative for a Bundesliga match — on both mobile and desktop – using dynamic creative. However, having the correct programmatic creative technology is essential for dynamic creative to succeed. A combination of a CMP, demand side platform (DSP), and data management platform (DMP) is recommended to build the ad variations required simply and rapidly.

**Creative optimization in real time (DCO)**

The next stage of dynamic creative is dynamic creative optimization. It is currently the most effective mix of programmatic creative tools accessible to display ad marketers. Marketers can use DCO to optimize and personalize the optimal creative mix for a certain audience segment. These ad versions may be readily generated and optimized in real-time using a CMP, resulting in improved ad performance and relevancy. However, there are several forms of DCO inside DCO! Template-based DCO, for example, is manually coded and pre-programmed. This means that while adverts can be generated in real-time, only text and graphics respond to user data. This can be quite effective, but it frequently results in bland advertising with product feeds and little else. DCO with a CMP is the pinnacle of programmatic creativity. When used in conjunction with a DCO platform, a CMP allows for more creative ad concepts and the utilization of a variety of ad versions. In-banner video and other interactive features, for example. Through innovative ad design, DCO with a CMP offers increased creative control and effect.

Printed in Great Britain
by Amazon

84471660R00084